The Inner Hater

HOW TO OVERCOME INSECURITY IN A
SOCIAL MEDIA WORLD

DeMarquis R. Battle

Battle 4 Christ Publishing, LLC
LANSING, MI

Battle Leadership Group LLC
P.O. Box 81189
Lansing, MI 48908
www.battleleadershipgroup.com

BATTLE
LEADERSHIP GROUP LLC
BATTLE **4** CHRIST PUBLISHING, LLC

The Inner Hater: How to Overcome Insecurity in a
Social Media World
ISBN 978-0692663721

Contents

Contents

I dedicate this book to every youth and young adult struggling with the challenges of social media. I want you to know your worth is not found in an app or website. Your worth is found in something greater. It is found in someone greater.

Darkness cannot drive out darkness; only light can do that. Hate cannot drive out hate; only love can do that.

—MARTIN LUTHER KING, JR.

CHAPTER 1

Hater Recognize

Have you ever read someone's status on Facebook or Twitter and wished it were yours? Have you looked at someone's picture on Instagram and felt disgust toward that individual? Have you ever gotten mad because a friend or co-worker was blessed with a new car and you are still driving that old 1990s Buick? Have you been passed over for the promotion by persons who seem less qualified? Have you ever witnessed a couple get married in the most beautiful wedding, but all you can think about is how you are single? What about that young adult who goes on exotic vacations across the globe. Does this upset you?

These are all real emotions, and if unchecked, can lead you down a very dark path of jealousy, envy, and strife. The first step to defeating these feelings is to know they exist. You must acknowledge they are real. You have to recognize the inner hater.

People do not like to think they are operating as a hater on the inside, but it's true. Sin makes us this way. Due to the fallen nature of humanity, and without accepting the redemptive work of Calvary, we do not have the capacity to live without hate. Our fleshly nature and attitude rule us. We innately display egotistical behavior and prideful symptoms that are diametrically opposed to godly character. But as in any addiction, negative stigma, or bad behavior, it must be realized. Once it is truly acknowledged, it can be dealt with. The problem with most of us is we are stuck in a state of denial.

First, we tell ourselves that we are not hating on the people we see on social media as all of their accomplishments flash across the virtual timeline, but rather we are just observing the difference(s) in our lives versus theirs. In some respects, this sounds reasonable. I mean, how can one totally shut his or her eyes to what others have accomplished and obtained, especially when many of us have failed to start that project we feel called to do? Well, it depends on which set of eyes you are looking with.

When we look with our natural eyes, we are observing the situation with our natural mind. In this perspective, there is nothing but flesh. Our observation becomes skewed when we look at people this way. In regards to the other set of eyes, we must begin to look in the Spirit. It's a counter cultural process. It enables us to see others who have been blessed, look well off, and are favored, with a joyful perspective and not with envy. When we look with the eyes of Jesus Christ, we are supportive. We are genuinely happy for whoever is receiving the blessings of God, both material and spiritual. In short, we need eye surgery. We need the ability to see that there is an inner hater within ourselves. One that doesn't like when people succeed. One that covets what others have. One that wishes we could have that gift or talent without going through what that person did to get it. Second, we need eyes to see others with the proper perspective.

There is Biblical evidence for this. The prophet Samuel was sent to the house of Jesse to anoint the next King of Israel. During this anointing service, Samuel was reminded of something very critical dealing with sight. In 1 Samuel 16:7 (ESV), it states:

- But the Lord said to Samuel, "Do not look on his appearance or on the height of his stature, because I have rejected him. For the Lord sees not as man sees: man looks on the outward appearance, but the Lord looks on the heart."

We are to model this type of vision and behavior as Christians. We shouldn't be as concerned with a person's outer appearance; we should be concerned with their heart. This keeps our hating in check, because when we see things the way that God sees it, we can't help but to love. The narrative described in 1 Samuel ends beautifully. After Samuel looked upon all of the sons of Jesse, he asked if there were any other sons left. There was. His name was David. He was the youngest son and the keeper of the sheep. You might be the last in your family, or the least in your group, but when God sees you, He loves what He sees. He finds the best in you. As children of God and image bearers in the earth, we should exemplify the same vision. We must recognize the inner hater and ask God to change your eyes. Start looking at things differently. Start asking what is right with a thing instead of what is wrong with it.

Now that you understand the importance of how to view other people, it's time to get an understanding of how you should view yourself, and how the inner hater is designed to bring you into a place of low self-esteem.

CHAPTER 2

I Don't like Myself, but I Should

The longer we, as a generation, gaze into the virtual cloudiness of social media, the deeper we go into the abyss of low self-esteem. Slowly but surely, we make ourselves less valuable. We make ourselves unattractive. We subscribe to being simple. We no longer see the diamond we were designed to be, we only see brokenness. This is what it's like when we allow the inner hater to take control of our lives and dictate how we feel.

After scrolling through the internet—viewing all the pictures, all the statuses, all the updates on social media— all we can see is our faults. Young women compare themselves, particularly when it comes to the issue of weight compared to other women they see on Facebook. Young men look at the wealth and riches of successful entrepreneurs and, from this observation, we feel like less of a man and our confidence is weakened. Young mothers look at opportunities that have appeared to pass them by because of their current responsibility as caretaker. From this, they often feel that success will never come their way. Students who have dropped out of college feel worthless because others in their class went on to work in corporate America and they themselves are stuck in a neutral job with no career advancement in sight. These examples happen on a daily basis for many of the millennials across the globe. We, as a generation, declare that we don't like ourselves, but we should.

We should see the value that we possess as individuals and as a generation. We find in scripture that we (humanity) were made in the image and likeness of God. This means that we were made to look like God, not in a physical form, for God is a spirit, but in terms of character and commission. Just as God was able to create the world through the words He uttered, we have the creative power and ability to speak to situations and see things happen. The issue with this understanding, again, is the effects of sin. Our ability to see ourselves the way God sees us has been damaged. When we get on the internet and start the compare and contrast game, we are left feeling like dirt.

In some respects, the analogy of dirt isn't bad. It just needs to be tweaked. We shouldn't view dirt in a negative connotation, but we should understand we were made from the dust of the earth. We were made with something that seemed minuscule, but when God gets into a thing, it becomes great. When God shaped the dust of the earth into a human being, He breathed the breath of life into it. When this happened, we were no longer just dust. We were no longer just rubbish or debris. We were no longer dirt people; we were God people. When the breath of God, which is synonymous with the Holy Spirit, enters into our life, purpose is activated. Our callings are realized. Destiny seems obtainable. You were once nothing but dirt, but with Christ, you are someone significant. You are a force to be reckoned with. Shift your thoughts. Turn the focus from your faults to the glory of Jesus. For in Him nothing is impossible.

When I say you should like yourself, I do not mean you should believe you are perfect. That is the lie of social media, that there are people who are perfect in their appearance, perfect in their careers, perfect in all aspects of life. Social media is designed for you to live in a digital world and developing a digital self-esteem. It's fake. It's manufactured. It's not real. Liking yourself is having the proper perspective of whom you are. In order to have this perspective, you have to let go of what once held you captive. In this next chapter, we will highlight the importance of letting go of the past.

CHAPTER 3

Let Go of the Past

S top right there. I caught you. Trying to look back into your past. We get so tempted to peek into the times of our past that we rarely focus on our present, and have no frame of mind for our future. This is the gift and the curse of social media. It's great because we are able to store hundreds of pictures, videos, tweets, and statuses of things we did one, five, or even ten years ago. This makes for a great scrapbook when we experience positive things, but what happens when we look at moments of our past and they become reminders of our failure? Too often, we spend our time looking back and not moving forward.

There are a few areas that negatively impact us when we look into our past, none greater than relationships. How many times have you logged on your favorite social media site and played "ex-boyfriend or girlfriend stalker?" You go to these people's pages trying to see how they are doing in their current lives. They appear happier. They look better. They have families. They have houses. They have careers. From this you play the "what if" game. You say to yourself, "What if we would have stayed together?" or you say, "I shouldn't have broken up with him or her." When you do this, you cut off access into your future and the many possibilities that lay before you. This reminds me of a narrative in scripture, regarding Lot and his wife. The Bible tells us that God was set to destroy Sodom and Gomorrah, a city that was filled with iniquity. Although judgement was falling on this region, God sent a warning to Lot and his family. They received detailed instruction to leave the city immediately and to run into a safe haven, a place to move forward. The only stipulation of their departure was not to look back at the destruction. Things started well, as they began to run from their past, but something was pulling Lot's wife to look back. The pull of the past tried to keep her engaged in something that was going to be destroyed. Often times we feel as though what we had was better than where we are going. We desire the certainty of our past instead of the possibilities of our future.

Well, the story ends in tragedy. In Genesis 19:26, it says that Lot's wife looked back toward Sodom and Gomorrah and she was instantly turned into a pillar of salt. Sometimes when we look into our past, we get stuck right where we are. We can never truly go back into our yesterday, nor can we move forward into our tomorrow. We stay stuck in an unproductive today. We have to let go of the past.

This isn't the only instance in scripture that we look back into our past, wishing we were still there. The Bible says that God delivered the children of Israel out of Egypt. While they were in transition, they began to complain about their conditions. Numbers 11:5 says:

- We remember the fish we ate in Egypt that cost nothing, the cucumbers, the melons, the leeks, the onions, and the garlic."

Though they had just been delivered from the oppressive hand of Pharaoh, the challenge of transition distorted their view of life. In reality, they were ten times better off walking in the desert of transition than being enslaved in their past. The children of Israel were delusional. The food items described were common in Egypt, but it was certainly not free. They paid for it with every lash on their back. They paid for it with every brick laid. They paid for it with every hour spent in fear and intimidation.

For many in our generation, we think because our current situation is not what we imagined, than our past may have been better. In actuality, you were a slave. You were chained emotionally to that bad relationship where physical or verbal abuse was the standard. You were a prisoner to your mistakes, always being reminded of how you messed up. You were captive to thoughts that were contrary to your purpose. Statements like, "You can't dream that big," or "You will never amount to anything."

As we continue in the Exodus narrative, we find that eventually the children of Israel made it to Canaan—the land that flowed with milk and honey. Their complaint extended a possible ten-day journey to a forty-year lesson. Do you want to delay the next phase of your life? Do you want to take a forty-year class on how to trust God and how to leave your past? Or, will you embrace the transition? Will you accept the past for what it was, a series of experiences both good and bad that helped to shape who you are today? A person who has learned from their mistakes and was appreciative of their failures and victories because, through it all, a greater testimony has been birthed.

Let go of the past and embrace the future. Your story is far from over. God has just begun to do the impossible in your life. Your future is a place filled with purpose and destiny. Once you commit to this new way of living, you must begin to speak differently. In the next chapter, we will learn how to develop a new language and how to keep that low self-esteem out of your heart and mind.

CHAPTER 4

Speak a New Language

Sticks and stones may break my bones but words will never hurt me. That is a lie. What you say does have an effect on you and others. The Bible says in Proverbs 18:21:

- Death and life are in the power of the tongue, and those who love it will eat its fruits.

What impact do your social media posts have on your readers? Better yet, what are you saying to yourself that impacts your ability to be successful? If, as a generation, we are going to overcome insecurity in this crazy social media world, we have to begin speaking a new language.

What does that look like? It is the language of positivity. If you suffer from low self-esteem, let's begin to combat that felling by declaring positive things over yourself. This is when the power kicks in. Life is administered when you speak well. When you don't, death is present. I am not referring to physical death, but to one that destroys your self-esteem. It destroys your ability to be confident in yourself. When we talk negative, we think negative. Even just in joking. Have you ever "clowned" on yourself? When I say this, I mean have you ever made fun of yourself in order to remove the pressure of meeting the societal standard? We do this all the time. We look into the mirror and say we look like a pig because we are maybe a bit more round in shape than others are. Perhaps we jokingly say that we are as dark as oil (my brothers and sisters of African descent who have struggled with the color of their skin know what I am referring to). Even those in the African-American community who are what we call "light-skinned," have also dealt with issues of low self-esteem or negative stigmas in regard to their skin tone. As if a negative attitude is synonymous with a color. For all who have said negative things to make themselves feel better or to put others down, you have to quit.

Begin loving yourself. These subtle attempts to lessen the pressure of living up to social media standards have damaging ramifications. It slowly peels away your confidence. Instead of speaking negatively, turn the table and say something nice. Not your standard of what nice or good is, but God's standard—which is scripture.

It is one thing to speak positively over ourselves with our own words, but it's something entirely different when we bathe in the richness of God's word and what He has to say about us. In the back of this book, you will be able to rehearse several scriptures geared to enhance your self-esteem and confidence. For now, one verse of scripture that speaks exactly to this is found in Psalms 139:13-14. It states:

- For you formed my inward parts; you knitted me together in my mother's womb. I praise you, for I am fearfully and wonderfully made. Wonderful are your works; my soul knows it very well.

This scripture shows the creative power of God and His personal involvement in who we are as people. He was the one who developed our inward parts. Even at the onset of our creative process, God was there ensuring every cell connected to the corresponding cell, and that our future would be one of blessing. Our response to this interaction from our mother's womb should be that of praise because we know our identity. We are fearfully and wonderfully made.

When you know God's hand has been on you even before your father knew your mother, you have a different view of who you are and *whose* you are. Start speaking the word of God every day until you can confidently say you believe it. Let your words align with God's thought about you. If you speak differently, you think differently. Ultimately, you will act differently. You will no longer seek the approval of man, but the approval of God. In the next chapter, we will discuss how to stop being an attention seeker on social media and how to use that platform for the purpose of God in your life.

CHAPTER 5

Attention Seekers

C hildren are precious, but they are also vulnerable. They need a certain amount of care and attention swung their way. In my experience, it doesn't take much for them to seek out your attention. As a father, I often deal with both of my children fighting to get into my face. If I compliment one child for their excellent form in brushing their teeth, the other child inquires if they are also doing a great job. If I clap my hands in approval for one of my children eating all their vegetables, my other child will scarf down the food on their plate to receive equal praise. They both desire my time and my approval. They have a need for my attention. Unfortunately, this "attention seeking" does not go away as we get older. If anything, it gets worse. As a generation, we seek attention from people to fill the void of a father. The problem is man can't fill this void. Only our Heavenly Father can.

This issue of attention seeking is magnified through the lens of social media. How many times have you been on Facebook or Twitter and have seen the most obvious posts for attention? This can be quite concerning, as many people air out their personal business in the virtual streets of social media. I grew up old school, so I can remember my mother saying, "Never share family business outside of this house." She wasn't just speaking of a physical address, but rather the four walls that encased the dynamics of our family. You don't share certain things with people who could potentially damage those who make up your family, especially when those things are being worked on "in-house." This certainly excludes situations that are abusive in nature, both physically and emotionally. If that is the case, professional help is encouraged, but I'm talking about the things that cause confusion for yourself and others.

People have mistaken social media as a diary of sorts. They post to the world the intimate areas of their life. It is no longer just a simple status update; it has become a post seeking attention. These types of tweets and posts resemble low self-esteem. The language is often negative, depressing, and alarming. Have you ever posted something that falls within that category? If so, you may be seeking attention and you don't even know it. What happens in these cases is you type up a post for social media and you find yourself refreshing the screen to see if anyone has responded. You're looking to see if anyone cares. This isn't exclusive to negative things. How many times have you posted a positive comment about something you've done or something great that happened in your life and you waited to see if anyone would commend you for that act? This is a generational problem. We seek approval. We seek praise. We seek attention. We thrive on it. We feed on it. It has become the air to our digital world. It's how we breathe on social media. This type of behavior is dangerous. The amount of attention seeking posts uploaded throughout a day, a week, or a year is nauseating. As quickly as we receive attention, the attention quickly shifts to someone or something else. This is why you can't put your faith in man alone. Things are always changing in the virtual world, therefore, put your desire on something that is everlasting. The Bible tells us to seek after something greater. Proverbs 8:17 says:

- I love those who love me, and those who seek me diligently find me.

If you are going to seek after anything in this life, let it be our Heavenly Father. His love is available. It doesn't ignore you like those on social media. God's love doesn't bluff. But others do when they "like" your post or "heart" your picture to pump you up. They may not even like you or your post. Beware of false comments made on social media. Your haters keep track of you seeking attention on social media. You see it when they post positive re-marks on your account when, in actuality, they se-cretly despise you. Not only this, but also many people just have trigger fingers. They hit the like and share buttons without a conscience. They do it just because. This is the deception of social media. The inner hater is slick. He would love you to continue seeking both good and bad attention on social media, so when you build up your digital sandcastle, he can come and knock it down with waves of criticism. Those waves are statements like, "I told you she wouldn't make it," or "There she go again, trying to be cute." Once inconvenience or tragedy hits your life, those same followers that "liked" your status are watching your fall with no words of encouragement and no words of motiva-tion. They have moved on to something more con-venient. This is why you can't put your faith into virtual friends that are merely acquaintances. The Bible says something interesting in regards to true friendship. Proverbs 18:24 states:

- A man of many companions may come to ruin, but there is a friend who sticks closer than a brother.

Another version says that unreliable friends mess each other up, but a real friend can be closer than your own brother can. What a statement. Stop mak-ing those on social media and even those in your physical existence more than who they are meant to be. Some people will never cross over into being a brother or sister in your life. People let you down, but Jesus said He would never leave you or forsake you. If you shift your attention from people to God then you're cooking something.

Imagine, instead of posting statuses that seek the attention of man, you share statuses that lift up the name of Jesus, thus generating the curiosity of others to seek your Lord and savior. You want this platform. You don't use social media for only selfish reasons or as a sounding board for all of life's troubles. You flip the script. You allow your witness and testimony to be shared for the glory of God. You filter your words to ensure there isn't selfish ambition involved and you ask God what you should share. This is how you effectively use the tool that has been created. A medium that reaches across the globe. In the next chapter, we will share how to loosen the grip social media may have on your life.

CHAPTER 6

Virtual Detox

Social media can be addicting. It has a death grip on us. If you have ever woken up and the first thing you do is check your Facebook or Twitter accounts, ladies and gentlemen, you have a problem. Just admit it. You spend way too much time on social media. You may need a virtual detox.

I committed to taking a break from social media after realizing I was spending more time using the technology than I was spending time with God. In other words, there was an unfruitful habit forming. I was lifting social media to a higher place than my relationship with Jesus Christ. It was taking over as the top priority each day. As an entrepreneur, marketing is often the lifeline to your business. Therefore, social media engagement seems like a necessity. In most instances, yes, you must interact with the virtual world, as it provides the greatest reach, but not at the expense of the true relationships that matter.

Have you fallen into this trap? Do you feel like you're missing something if you don't check Twitter every hour? Trust me; it will still be there in a few days if you decide to put it down for a season. As I began to reflect on this idea of a virtual detox, I started thinking about what Jesus' goal was when He died on the cross. It was to bring us back into right relationship with the Father. The shed blood of Jesus provides the remission of our sin, and the barrier that once stood between God and man has been removed. We can now enter freely into the presence of God and interact with Him. This is known as our vertical relationship.

There is nothing standing in the way of a person who desires to communicate with the Lord. The only thing that stops us is our willingness to put things in the way. This is what social media does when it's not positioned correctly. Our spiritual pathway gets clogged by Instagram and Periscope. It hinders the flow of the spirit to reach our hearts for transformation. Not only does our vertical relationship get messed up, but our horizontal relationships also take a hit.

For me, social media was starting to become a strategy the enemy used to separate my family. I don't want to exaggerate, as if my marriage was on the rocks, but there were small things upsetting the apple cart, so to speak. Things like having your cell phone out at dinnertime, or instead of having a conversation with your spouse about your day, you are plugged in, trying to find out the latest sports score. Albeit subtle, the small things hindered many from doing and accomplishing the great things.

So how did I change my priorities? I simply put my phone down. I ignored the chirps and chimes that go off when I receive a new notification. I started small and took a few days to stay off Facebook so I could focus on what really mattered. My vertical and horizontal relationships. What I found was that I really didn't miss it too much. Yes, I enjoy social media, but I didn't need to take it with me everywhere. With anything you try to fast from, which is a form of spiritual discipline, you have to replace it with something that will help you while you abstain. I used the word of God. When I felt the urge to look at social media, I went to my Bible app instead. I worshiped the Lord. I was able to rest in His presence. I realized the clog in the spirit that was once a hindrance was now being pushed out of the way. The flow of the sprit was smoother. I wasn't glued to YouTube or following my news feed. I was enjoying God and my family.

The other good thing about a virtual detox is that when you decide to come back, you are able to post more things of significance. Your mind is clearer. Perhaps God has done something new in your life worth mentioning. People can become numb to your voice if you are posting all the time and a break allows expectation to build. That's if you have a platform to reach people and not just fill their time-line with junk.

Do you need a detox? Decide today that you will not let social media bog you down. Declare freedom from the chain on your wrist that connects to your cell phone. Close your laptop. Turn off your computer and shift your focus to things that are more important. Let your vertical relationship with God and your horizontal relationships with your spouse, your children, your extended family, and friends be the priority.

CHAPTER 7

Scripture Affirmations

Below you will find scripture references that will affirm your spirit and build your self-esteem. Begin reciting these scriptures daily and watch the Lord transform and renew your mind.

- **1 Samuel 16:7** - But the LORD said to Samuel, "Do not look on his appearance or on the height of his stature, because I have rejected him. For the LORD sees not as man sees: man looks on the outward appearance, but the LORD looks on the heart."

- **1 Peter 3:3-4** - Do not let your adorning be external—the braiding of hair and the putting on of gold jewelry, or the clothing you wear—but let your adorning be the hidden person of the heart with the imperishable beauty of a gentle and quiet spirit, which in God's sight is very precious.

- **Joshua 1:9** - Have I not commanded you? Be strong and courageous. Do not be frightened, and do not be dismayed, for the LORD your God is with you wherever you go.

- **Jeremiah 29:11** – "For I know the plans I have for you," declares the LORD, "plans for welfare and not for evil, to give you a future and a hope."

- **Genesis 1:27** - So God created man in his own image, in the image of God he created him; male and female he created them.

- **Isaiah 41:10** - Fear not, for I am with you; be not dismayed, for I am your God; I will strengthen you, I will help you, I will uphold you with my righteous right hand.

ABOUT THE AUTHOR

DeMarquis R. Battle is the founder and president of Battle Leadership Group LLC. He is an author, educator, entrepreneur, pastor, and speaker. He holds an M.A. in Ministry Studies from Grace College & Seminary and an M.A. in Bible & Theology from Lincoln Christian University. His mission is to help the next generation walk in their purpose and destiny.